CAPTIVITY

TOI
DERRICOTTE

CAPTIVITY

University of Pittsburgh Press

Published by the University of Pittsburgh Press, Pittsburgh, Pa. 15260
Copyright © 1989, Toi Derricotte
All rights reserved
Baker & Taylor International, London
Manufactured in the United States of America

Library of Congress Cataloging-in-Publication Data

Derricotte, Toi, 1941–
    Captivity / Toi Derricotte.
        p.   cm. — (Pitt poetry series)
    ISBN 0-8229-3628-3. — ISBN 0-8229-5422-2 (pbk.)
    I. Title.   II. Series.
PS3554.E73C37   1989
811'.54—dc20   89-31840
                                                CIP

The author and publisher wish to express their grateful acknowledgment to
the following publications in which some of these poems first appeared:
American Poetry Review ("Touching/Not Touching: My Mother"); *The
Beloit Poetry Journal* ("Tiedown"); *The Black Scholar* ("The Furious Boy");
Callaloo ("Fears of the Eighth Grade," "Hamtramck: The Polish Women,"
"Letter to Miss Glazer," and "A Note on My Son's Face"); *The Caribbean
Writer* ("The Choice" and "Plaid Pants"); *Footwork Magazine* ("Stuck");
Ironwood ("The Friendship"); *The Massachusetts Review* ("Blackbottom"
and "The Struggle"); *Michigan Quarterly Review* ("Aerial Photographs Be-
fore the Atomic Bomb"); *New England Review and Bread Loaf Quarterly*
("Christmas Eve: My Mother Dressing"); *New Letters* ("Books"); *Open
Places* ("Poem for My Father"); *Painted Bride Quarterly* ("Squeaky Bed");
Pequod ("The Promise" and "Saturday Night"); *Poetry East* ("Before Making
Love," "My Father Still Sleeping After Surgery," and "The Polishers of
Brass"); *U.S. 1 Worksheets* ("Allen Ginsberg"); and *Woman Poet: The East*
("The Testimony of Sister Maureen").

"The Good Old Dog" and "On Stopping Late in the Afternoon for Steamed
Dumplings" first appeared in *An Introduction to Poetry*, 3rd ed., ed. Louis
Simpson (St. Martin's Press, 1986).

The writing of these poems was aided by a fellowship from The National
Endowment for the Arts and a grant from the Maryland State Arts Council.

*The publication of this book is supported by grants
from the National Endowment for the Arts
in Washington, D.C., a Federal agency,
and the Pennsylvania Council on the Arts.*

For my family

"[According to] the legend of the Lamed Vav Zaddikin . . . *there are people in the world who absorb the suffering and the evil. They don't even know that this is what they are doing but because of their existence, the world continues. The problem with this role is that, almost invariably, they are consumed by it."* —Jerome Groopman, M.D., The Washington Post

"But even when I am at a loss to define
the essence of freedom
I know full well the meaning
of captivity."
—Adam Zagajewski
Translated by Antony Graham

Contents

Contents

I.
BLACKBOTTOM

The Minks

In the backyard of our house on Norwood,
there were five hundred steel cages lined up,
each with a wooden box
roofed with tar paper;
inside, two stories, with straw
for a bed. Sometimes the minks would pace
back and forth wildly, looking for a way out;
or else they'd hide in their wooden houses, even when
we'd put the offering of raw horse meat on their trays, as if
they knew they were beautiful
and wanted to deprive us.
In spring the placid kits
drank with glazed eyes.
Sometimes the mothers would go mad
and snap their necks.
My uncle would lift the roof like a god
who might lift our roof, look down on us
and take us out to safety.
Sometimes one would escape.
He would go down on his hands and knees,
aiming a flashlight like
a bullet of light, hoping to catch
the orange gold of its eyes.
He wore huge boots, gloves
so thick their little teeth couldn't bite through.
"They're wild," he'd say. "Never trust them."
Each afternoon when I put the scoop of raw meat rich
with eggs and vitamins on their trays,
I'd call to each a greeting.
Their small thin faces would follow as if slightly curious.
In fall they went out in a van, returning
sorted, matched, their skins hanging down on huge metal
hangers, pinned by their mouths.
My uncle would take them out when company came

and drape them over his arm—the sweetest cargo.
He'd blow down the pelts softly
and the hairs would part for his breath
and show the shining underlife which, like
the shining of the soul, gives us each
character and beauty.

Blackbottom

When relatives came from out of town,
we would drive down to Blackbottom,
drive slowly down the congested main streets
    —Beubian and Hastings—
trapped in the mesh of Saturday night.
Freshly escaped, black middle class,
we snickered, and were proud;
the louder the streets, the prouder.
We laughed at the bright clothes of a prostitute,
a man sitting on a curb with a bottle in his hand.
We smelled barbecue cooking in dented washtubs,
    and our mouths watered.
As much as we wanted it we couldn't take the chance.

Rhythm and blues came from the windows, the throaty voice of
    a woman lost in the bass, in the drums, in the dirty down
    and out, the grind.
"I love to see a funeral, then I know it ain't mine."
We rolled our windows down so that the waves rolled over us
    like blood.
We hoped to pass invisibly, knowing on Monday we would
    return safely to our jobs, the post office and classroom.
We wanted our sufferings to be offered up as tender meat,
and our triumphs to be belted out in raucous song.
We had lost our voice in the suburbs, in Conant Gardens,
    where each brick house delineated a fence of silence;
we had lost the right to sing in the street and damn creation.

We returned to wash our hands of them,
to smell them
whose very existence
tore us down to the human.

Poem for My Father

You closed the door.
I was on the other side,
screaming.

It was black in your mind.
Blacker than burned-out fire.
Blacker than poison.

Outside everything looked the same.
You looked the same.
You walked in your body like a living man.
But you were not.

would you not speak to me for weeks
would you hang your coat in the closet without saying hello
would you find a shoe out of place and beat me
would you come home late
would i lose the key
would you find my glasses in the garbage
would you put me on your knee
would you read the bible to me in your smoking jacket after
    your mother died
would you come home drunk and snore
would you beat me on the legs
would you carry me up the stairs by my hair so that my feet
    never touch bottom
would you make everything worse
to make everything better

i believe in god, the father almighty,
the maker of heaven, the maker
of my heaven and my hell.

would you beat my mother
would you beat her till she cries like a rabbit
would you beat her in a corner of the kitchen
while i am in the bathroom trying to bury my head underwater
would you carry her to the bed

would you put cotton and alcohol on her swollen head
would you make love to her hair
would you caress her hair
would you rub her breasts with ben gay until she stinks
would you sleep in the other room in the bed next to me while
    she sleeps on the pull-out cot
would you come on the sheet while i am sleeping. later i look
    for the spot
would you go to embalming school with the last of my mother's
    money
would i see your picture in the book with all the other
    black boys you were the handsomest
would you make the dead look beautiful
would the men at the elks club
would the rich ladies at funerals
would the ugly drunk winos on the street
know ben
pretty ben
regular ben

would your father leave you when you were three with a mother
    who threw butcher knives at you
would he leave you with her screaming red hair
would he leave you to be smothered by a pillow she put
    over your head
would he send for you during the summer like a rich uncle
would you come in pretty corduroys until you were nine and
    never heard from him again

would you hate him
would you hate him every time you dragged hundred pound
    cartons of soap down the stairs into white ladies' basements
would you hate him for fucking the woman who gave birth to you
hate him flying by her house in the red truck so that the
    other father threw down his hat in the street and stomped
    on it angry like we never saw him

7

(bye bye
to the will of grandpa
bye bye to the family fortune
bye bye when he stomped that hat,
to the gold watch,
embalmer's palace,
grandbaby's college)
mother crying silently, making floating island
sending it up to the old man's ulcer

would grandmother's diamonds
close their heartsparks
in the corner of the closet
like the yellow eyes of cockroaches?

Old man whose sperm swims in my veins,

come back in love, come back in pain.

Christmas Eve: My Mother Dressing

My mother was not impressed with her beauty;
once a year she put it on like a costume,
plaited her black hair, slick as cornsilk, down past her hips,
in one rope-thick braid, turned it, carefully, hand over hand,
and fixed it at the nape of her neck, stiff and elegant as a crown,
with tortoise pins, like huge insects,
some belonging to her dead mother,
some to my living grandmother.
Sitting on the stool at the mirror,
she applied a peachy foundation that seemed to hold her down,
    to trap her,
as if we never would have noticed what flew among us unless
    it was weighted and bound in its mask.
Vaseline shined her eyebrows,
mascara blackened her lashes until they swept down like feathers;
her eyes deepened until they shone from far away.

Now I remember her hands, her poor hands, which, even then
    were old from scrubbing,
whiter on the inside than they should have been,
and hard, the first joints of her fingers, little fattened pads,
the nails filed to sharp points like old-fashioned ink pens,
    painted a jolly color.
Her hands stood next to her face and wanted to be put away,
    prayed
for the scrub bucket and brush to make them useful.
And, as I write, I forget the years I watched her
pull hairs like a witch from her chin, magnify
every blotch—as if acid were thrown from the inside.

But once a year my mother
rose in her white silk slip,
not the slave of the house, the woman,

9

took the ironed dress from the hanger—
allowing me to stand on the bed, so that
my face looked directly into her face,
and hold the garment away from her
as she pulled it down.

The House on Norwood

That brick bungalow
rose out of the storm
of racism like an ark.
We found a way—the post office workers,
the teachers, principals—we found
a nest, a mile of wilderness,
and farmed the bones of our children
out of it. Suburban, up
from the South, our boys
not shot, our girls not pregnant
with belly after belly
of welfare children.
No matter how I hated and feared
the rages, the silences,
we did grow
iron bones.

I'd wake on cold dark mornings
earlier than the packing of the factory lunchpails,
my father breathing
like an engine, my mother next to him, almost
invisible,
my leg over the crib rail, quietly,
slowly,
down the stairs in my wet cold pants,
padding through the living room, the dining room, the hall,
to where she lay,
my Aunt Lenora,
warm, still sleeping, who
hid me when my father came—
"Is Toi in there?" She'd lie.
I'd crawl under the sheet,
sneak her nightdress up around
her thighs and peek.
She'd snore, limp, trusting.

St. Peter Claver

Every town with black Catholics has a St. Peter Claver's.
My first was nursery school.
Miss Maturin made us fold our towels in a regulation square
  and nap on army cots.
No mother questioned; no child sassed.
In blue pleated skirts, pants, and white shirts,
we stood in line to use the open toilets
and conserved light by walking in darkness.
Unsmiling, mostly light-skinned, we were the children of the
  middle class, preparing to take our parents' places in a
  world that would demand we fold our hands and wait.
They said it was good for us, the bowl of soup, its
  pasty whiteness;
I learned to swallow and distrust my senses.

On holy cards St. Peter's face is olive-toned, his hair
  near kinky;
I thought he was one of us who pass between the rich and poor,
  the light and dark.
Now I read he was "a Spanish Jesuit priest who labored for
  the salvation of the African Negroes and the abolition
  of the slave trade."
I was tricked again, robbed of my patron,
and left with a debt to another white man.

The Weakness

That time my grandmother dragged me
through the perfume aisles at Saks, she held me up
by my arm, hissing, "Stand up,"
through clenched teeth, her eyes
bright as a dog's
cornered in the light.
She said it over and over,
as if she were Jesus,
and I were dead. She had been
solid as a tree,
a fur around her neck, a
light-skinned matron whose car was parked, who walked
  on swirling
marble and passed through
brass openings—in 1945.
There was not even a black
elevator operator at Saks.
The saleswoman had brought velvet
leggings to lace me in, and cooed,
as if in the service of all grandmothers.
My grandmother had smiled, but not
hungrily, not like my mother
who hated them, but wanted to please,
and they had smiled back, as if
they were wearing wooden collars.
When my legs gave out, my grandmother
dragged me up and held me like God
holds saints by the
roots of the hair. I begged her
to believe I couldn't help it. Stumbling,
her face white
with sweat, she pushed me through the crowd, rushing

away from those eyes
that saw through
her clothes, under
her skin, all the way down
to the transparent
genes confessing.

Fires in Childhood

I. Aerial Photographs Before the Atomic Bomb

Why did such terrible events
catch my eye? After Hiroshima,
I turned the picture in *Life* around
in circles, trying to figure out this huge
wheel in the middle of the air, how it
turned, a ferris wheel, its lights
burning like eyes.
The atom spinning
on course over the sleeping,
vulnerable planet. I turned it the way one might
turn a kaleidoscope or prism. Even then I
knew about the town lying under,
like a child sleeping under the
watchful gaze of a rapist, before the spasm
of stopped breath, the closure at the
scream of the throat, before the body is awakened
along its shocked spine to bursting
light, the legs closing, the arms,
like a chilled flower. That eye, that spinning eye

seeking the combustible.
This was a heat
I had felt already in our house on Norwood.
                                    Everything
looked green, placid as a green field,
predictable as machinery—an antique clock.
This was the instant
before destruction,
the fiery atom stuck
as if under the control of the artist
before it spilled and became irretrievable.
Could it be sucked back
in its lead bag, the doors of the underbelly slammed,

15

and those men who went on to
suicide and madness, go on instead
to become lovers, priests, Buddhist
smilers and scholars, gardeners in the small plots
of contained passion?

II. The Chicago Streetcar Fire

. . . burning out of the
center of the *Free Press,* its peeling paint
crackling like paper.
I hid the pictures from my mother, needing to see
those who were fried in an
iron skillet, the men, women, children
melted together in a crust of skin,
a blackened hand more dense
than charred steak, as if it had been
forgotten in the fire years. They crammed together
at the exit as if terror could
leap through locked doors.
Only a fraction of an inch
from safety! Maybe if one had
gone the other way—
blood going up in flames
like gasoline, heads torches.
Children who did not
escape their childhoods—

        Feathers!   Ash!

Abuse

Mama, the janitor is kissing me. Don't tell me that, you make me suffer. You always make me suffer. Mama, father is beating me. Don't tell me that. What do you want me to do? Mama, the janitor is coming in the house and wants to feel me. Well, come here, come see the janitor and say hello. I come in a starched pinafore and she stands at the foot of the stairs as if she is proud. Where were you when a man, a man who could fix a toy, stuck his tongue in my mouth and rubbed his thing on my school uniform? When I flew up the stairs into the arms of the Blessed Mother, where were you? Wanting to bury your head in a tub of warm water, heating dinner in your slip and socks with half a can of flat beer. Where were you when he came with his fists, after nights of "yes suh boss" and "no suh boss," when he knocked us around and threw meat on the table? Mama doesn't care. She puts her little hands in the air and it still comes raining down. Everything's neatly in place— every pin, every needle—but the walls are coming apart. Roaches peek out of the cracks, their feelers trembling; and the little girl is wiped across the floor like a flour sack. She is decorated by love. Her legs have stripes from beating. Later her father sponges her eyes where tears spill like blood. She shuts down like a factory—every thought, a hand without a way to work—or lies in the dark like a whipped dog praying he'll come.

High School

I didn't want to be
bunched with the black girls in the back
of Girls Catholic Central's cafeteria.
They were my kin,
but sitting there I was aware
of that invisible wall, the others
circling us like stars. The others:

Gintare,
the Ukrainian with limbs like silk and childbearing hips.
Kathleen, who would be a nun, whose mother saw the Virgin in
    the suburbs.
Pignalls, whose body had grown into a giant's, who towered
    over the gold prom queens, not like a man, but a child who
    had grown into a monster, her broken speech a path out of
    herself she could not follow.
Donna, her hair hanging over her face like a veil—her knees
    made for kneeling, her stomach for fasts, her genitals for
    the loneliness of the cot, but the rest of her unable to hold
    up holiness.
Jo, who let boys penetrate and shrugged off other wisdoms;
    her long eyelashes held grains of sand, as if tiny pieces of
    eternity were working themselves through her.
Lenore, whose square body threatened the narrow pews;
    expelled, who lived in the back of a White Tower with her
    first woman lover.
Marty, whose palate and teeth stuck out, like some hairy
    specimen of our ancestors, alone with her mother, sleeping
    on the pull-out cot.

None of them called me nigger;
but they were ignorant
as God of our suffering.

19

Hamtramck: The Polish Women

Handwritten margin notes: Even beautiful women cannot escape their role of women. Their role of women.

What happens to the beautiful girls with slender hips and
   bright round dresses?
One day they disappear without leaving a trace of themselves,
and the next they appear again, dragging a heavy
   shopping cart from the bakery to the pork store with
   packages of greasy sausage and potatoes.
Like old nuns they waddle down the main street, past the rich
   gaudy cathedral with the little infant of Prague—in
   real clothes—linens they tend lovingly, starch in
   steamy buckets (their hands thick as potatoes, white),
   and iron with dignity.

The Struggle

We didn't want to be white—or did we?
What did we want?
In two bedrooms, side by side,
four adults, two children.
My aunt and uncle left before light.
My father went to the factory, then the cleaners.
My mother vacuumed, ironed, cooked,
pasted war coupons. In the afternoon
she typed stencils at the metal kitchen table.
I crawled under pulling on her skirt.
What did we want?
As the furniture became modern, the carpet deep, the white
ballerina on the mantel lifted her arms like some girl near
terror;
the Degas ballerinas bowed softly in a group, a gray sensual
beauty.
What did we push ourselves out of ourselves
to do? Our hands
on the doors, cooking utensils, keys; our hands
folding the paper money, tearing the bills.

II.
RED ANGEL

"True revolution happens when you love."
—Ché Guevara

Before Making Love

I move my hands over your face,
closing my eyes, as if blind;
the cheek bones, broadly spaced,
the wide thick nostrils of the African,
the forehead whose bones push
at both sides as if the horns
of fallen angels lie just under,
the chin that juts forward with pride.
I think of the delicate skull of the Taung child—
earliest of human beings
emerged from darkness—whose geometry
brings word of a small town of dignity
that all the bloody kingdoms rest on.

[The Taung child is a fossil, a juvenile *Australopithecus africanus*,
from Taung, South Africa, two million years old.]

Saturday Night

We come home from the movie, and you head for the TV.
I peek out of the bathroom to hear you move around in there.
I'm screaming: "You're sick. I can't take it anymore.
   You've been with machines all day—computers, TV. You
   don't want anything to do with me."
You deny this. You had only gone into that room to put down
   your wallet.
I want to kill. Am crazed with the smell of my own blood.
"I don't need this. You think I need you like before?"
I hear you in the bathroom cutting your toenails, it takes a
   long time. I wonder if you are on the toilet.
"You're so used to me being the one to need you, it's a
   game. But games can be stopped," I scream.
I grab a magazine and get into bed, flipping through. I want
   to attack until I feel you in my hands, cut through to
   the other side, like diving toward a light.
Will you save me? Will you reach out your hand and save me?
   Just one finger on my arm . . .
You pull back the covers and come into bed, gazing up at
   the ceiling.
I want to touch you, but can't move. How can I stay in a room
   too small to stand or sit or lie in, cramped
   in a fetal posture?
I want to threaten until God takes back his lies of paradise,
   till the sun cracks open and lets us die.
We are packed in a frame bed like a child's wagon in the
   middle of a tornado.
"Games can be stopped," I repeat softly.

"I am so lonely," I say. "So lonely."

On Stopping Late in the Afternoon
for Steamed Dumplings

The restaurant is empty
except for the cooks and waiters.
One makes a pillow of linens
and sleeps, putting his feet up in a booth;
another folds paper tablecloths. Why
have I stopped to eat alone on this rainy
day? Why savor the wet meat of the
steamed dumpling? As I pick it up,
the waiter appraises me. Am I
one of those women who must stop
for treats along the way—am I that starved?
The white dough burns—much too hot—yet,
I stick it in my mouth, quickly,
as if to destroy the evidence.
The waiter still watches. Suddenly
I am sorry to be here, sad,
my little pleasure stolen.

Stuck

The traffic backs up.
We're not moving.
The CB says it's construction
on the bridge. "I should be driving," I say.
"I'm afraid to be stuck on a bridge."
"It's only a short one," you say,
"just over the Connecticut River."
I sit back on my backbone.
"Shouldn't you be in that lane? It
seems to be moving faster." "Yeah,
but the CB says the left lane
is open on the bridge."
We sit. The truckers are angry—
"Another four-wheeler messin' things up."
The four-wheelers are angry—
"Goddamn eighteen-wheelers fuckin' up the bridge."
The right lane moves ahead.
My heart pounds;
my palms glaze with sweat.
If I were driving, I say to myself, I'd
move into that fast lane, then
cut back in front of the others. You are
calm, humming, tapping the steering
wheel with your fingers—though the car
in front of us is letting drivers
cut back in.
"No cuts," I want to scream.
But I keep silent,
Zenlike, count
my breaths to thirteen
and start again.

Squeaky Bed

At your mother's house we lie
stiff in our bed as paper dolls.
Soon you snore and the crickets burst
through the window with squeaky horns.

She is old and toothless,
when we make love we
rock in the arms of a
new mother, she will not hear.

The crickets never sleep. All night
they want it.
Love is more real
than fear. Soon we will
give ourselves over to the noise.

The Good Old Dog

I will lay down my silk robe
beside me near the old bed,
for the good old dog;
             she loves the feel
of it under her, and she will
push it and pull it, knead
and scrape until she has it right;
             then she'll drop down,
heavy, silver and black in the moonlight,
on it and a couple of pillows (not
bothering the cat who has taken over
             her real bed)

                      and breathe out deeply.

Gorgeously fat,
her face
like the face of a seal.

The Promise

I will never again
expect too much of you. I have
found out the secret of marriage:
I must keep seeing your beauty
like a stranger's, like the face
of a young girl passing on a train
whose moment of knowing illumines
it—a golden letter in a book.
I will look at you in such
exaggerated moments, lengthening
one second and shrinking eternity
until they fit together like man and wife.
My pain is expectation:
I watch you for hours sleeping, expecting
you to roll over like a dead man
and look me in the eye;
my days are seconds of waiting
like the seconds between the makings
of boiling earth and sweating rivers.
What am I waiting for if not
your face—like a fish floating
up to the surface, a known
but forgotten expression that
suddenly appears—or like myself,
in a strip of mirror, when, having
passed, I come back to that image
hoping to find the woman
missing. Why do you think I sleep
in the other room, planets away,
in a darkness where I could die solitary,
an old nun wrapped in clean white sheets?
Because of lies I sucked
in my mother's milk, because
of pictures in my first grade reader—

families in solid towns as if
the world were rooted and grew down
holding to the rocks, eternally;
because of rings in jewelers' windows
engraved with sentiments—*I love you
forever*—as if we could survive
any beauty for longer than just after . . .
So I hobble down a hall
of disappointments past where
your darkness and my darkness have
had intercourse with each other.
Why have I wasted my life
in anger, thinking I could have more
than what is glimpsed in recognitions?
I will let go, as we must
let go of an angel called
back to heaven; I will not hold
her glittering robe, but let it
drift above me until I see
the last shred of evidence.

For a Man Who Speaks with Birds

Always, around the others
you wear your body
as if you put on the old
football pads of boyhood;
they are still much too large for you,
you turn and twist in them
like a man in the sheets of a nightmare.
Businessmen choose you to lead them,
you step forward
built for defenses—barreled ribs
around the heart of one
who wants to speak to the redbirds.
Are you trying to find a way out,
like a woman stuck between floors
pushing all the dead buttons?
Your mouth has spoken
the whistles of redbirds,
but your eyes know how to look
from a great height,
as a king must have watched
a slave from a window.

I pity you going from town to town
with your satchel of orders
from devil to devil;
your bones must hold up such metal
while your heart wants to speak
in the tongues of red angels.

The Friendship

I tell you I am angry.
You say you are afraid.
You take your glasses off and lay
them on the table like a sparkling weapon.
I hold my purse in front of me.
Do I love you? Do you love me?
"If we just had time . . ."

You could show me how you wore your hair
pushed forward over one eye, hiding
half of what you knew of beauty.

Poor friendship, why must it sit
at a table where the waitress
is ready to go home? In a city
between tunnels—cracks
of darkness in the sea.

Touching/Not Touching: My Mother

That first night in the hotel bedroom,
when the lights go out,
she is already sleeping (that woman who has always
claimed sleeplessness), inside her quiet breathing
like a long red gown. How can she
sleep? My heart beats as if I am alone,
for the first time, with a lover or a beast.
Will I hate her drooping mouth,
her old woman rattle? Once I nearly
suffocated on her breast. Now I can almost
touch the other side of my life.

ii.

Undressing
in the dark,
looking,
not looking,
we parade before each other,
old proud peacocks, in our stretch marks
with hanging butts. We are equals. No
more do I need to wear her high heels to step
inside the body of a woman.
Her beauty and strangeness no longer seduce
me out of myself. I show my good side, my
long back, strong mean legs, my thinness that
came from learning to hold back
from taking what's not mine. No more
a thief for love. She takes off her
bra, facing me, and I see those gorgeous
globes, soft, creamy,

high; my mouth waters.
how will I resist
crawling in beside her, putting
my hand for warmth under
her thin night dress?

Tiedown

They tie my father's hands and feet
to stop him from pulling his tubes out.
He punches the nurse and kicks her,
and they tie him tighter.
The body will get better
no matter how they have to hurt it.
Sitting up in his chair, he
sees only the top of a bare tree. Its
wild branches stick up
like suture hairs.

My Father Still Sleeping After Surgery

In spite of himself,
my father loved me. In spite
of the hands that beat me, in spite
of the mouth that kept silent, in spite
of the face that turned cruel
as a gold Chinese king,
he could not control the love
that came out of him.
The body is monumental, a colossus
through which he breathes.
His hands crawl over his stomach
jerkily as sand crabs on five legs;
he makes a fist
like the fist of a newborn.

III.

THE TESTIMONY OF SISTER MAUREEN

The Testimony of Sister Maureen

Sister Maureen Murphy, a teaching nun in the Rochester-based Sisters of St. Joseph, was arraigned in June 1976, on a charge of first-degree manslaughter in the death of her newborn son. In 1977, she was tried and declared not guilty.

"I know it matters if I'm convicted, but I've already imprisoned myself in my mind and heart. I'm imprisoned because I can't escape from my thoughts. I want to know if I harmed the child. I know I must have, because I was the only one there."
> —From a conversation with psychiatrist
> William Liberston on 20 May 1976.

1

i enter.

a woman leads me in,
red tiles and clerestory windows,
the sun bleeds in like beets;
"my daughter," she says
not kindly or unkindly, but as if
her tongue were tied,
her smile a deformity,
"sell your lover's heart for Christ."

we eat the blood-soaked stone, dislodge
thigh, crack dry skin in our teeth,

as if the grit of innocence must
match the muscle in our jaws.

2

my skin grows black.
i burn.
my eyes pale like lepers.
i wear goat fur, stink of sin
in the middle of their kindness.
under my hood,
i do not pray as they think—
my eyes turn pink with rage
clear as the nucleus of germ.
these are the works of God:
the miracle ignites Him in my bones.

3

the children in my care
with wisp-thin wings
like butterflies of glass
fly to the brown
floor of my shuttered room,
their music in my book
like a rush of wet sweet air.

i come down to meet them,
breathing in the iron corset, head
spinning loose and fragile,
floats like an angel in a starched white pinafore.

i rush with arms
to shut the gap.
fit airless bodies
in this chewed
curve of my spine.

4

a man comes in the bar,
this is a dream, it seems
to be a dream
how did i get
in this seaport town, how
did i trawl
this black lobster
with my own claw
how did i latch
him by the throat
and hand him my life?

i drink a beer, the glass
slick in my hand as sea,
the room smells of fog;
myself in a cotton dress,
the table top unwashed,
blurry as a drunk man's face

(where are my sisters
like bells they are
shivering in that dark tower)

he follows me,
a presence in the bushes
like an image in a black mirror

the moon breaks. his face
is ashes in the crowns of trees.

5

the air hums at night
the wings of bees
beg for entrance at my ears
return to the familiar nest
it is spring
this year there is a heart
at its center
red with thorns
He grinds me muscle thick
i cannot shut the singing out

6

one night   i place my ear
against the wall

                              sometimes

i hear Him
out there

                         sometimes

i feel Him

shake the floor
lonely as a devil

                         i
drive through darkness
in harness
                    look
not left
nor right
for fear

                        His eye
                        lidless and white
        watches

                                tonight
                        i hear
        no one
                        but
        blood
        seems
        singing out of veins,
                                veins
        cracking in the
        center of the
        plaster
        till
        all the halls
                        are white

        i
        have touched
        pain
        laid my hand
        on it
        and felt it
        climb like mountains
        in the air
                        tonight

        this
        demon
                        tears
        dark

                        45

out of the sky

i/

rise

i/

part

like skin

over

His goat heart

7

the child is dead
they bring him in a white boat
            to my bed
        like moses
        like the jew-child

i place him in the reeds
thickly hidden
in the salamander green
            and the brown bark

my stocking is around his neck

i am the maiden in the window
who watched him through the first

            bright

        ball of air

            triumphant
            as a god

                    i am

god/

     mother

            God
will take my place

IV.

THE TERRIBLE BRIGHT AIR

Boy at the Paterson Falls

I am thinking of that boy who bragged about the day he threw
   a dog over and watched it struggle to stay upright all
   the way down.
I am thinking of that rotting carcass on the rocks,
and the child with such power he could call to a helpless
   thing as if he were its friend, capture it, and think of
   the cruelest punishment.
It must have answered some need, some silent screaming in a
   closet, a motherless call when night came crashing;
it must have satisfied, for he seemed joyful, proud, as if he
   had once made a great creation out of murder.
That body on the rocks, its sharp angles, slowly took the shape of
   what was underneath, bones pounded, until it lay on the bottom
   like a scraggly rug.
Nothing remains but memory—and the suffering of those who
   would walk into the soft hands of a killer for a crumb of bread.

Fears of the Eighth Grade

When I ask what things they fear,
their arms raise like soldiers volunteering for battle:
Fear of going into a dark room, my murderer is waiting.
Fear of taking a shower, someone will stab me.
Fear of being kidnapped, raped.
Fear of dying in war.
When I ask how many fear this,
all the children raise their hands.

I think of this little box of consecrated land,
the bombs somewhere else,
the dead children in their mothers' arms,
women crying at the gates of the bamboo palace.

How thin the veneer!
The paper towels, napkins, toilet paper—everything
burned up in a day.

These children see the city after Armageddon.
The demons stand visible in the air
between their friends talking.
They see fire in a spring day
the instant before conflagration.
They feel blood through closed faucets,
the dead rising from the boiling seas.

The Furious Boy

In the classroom, the furious boy—a heavy star.
The unhappiness in the room finds his heart,
                    enters it;
The sheet of paper flapping in his face.
Who takes something takes it from him.

The rejections look for him.
The inflicted pain finds him.
He cannot say no. The hole in his heart deepens,
pain has no way out. A light too heavy
to escape, a presence more concentrated,
warmth is everywhere except where he sits at the center
holding the world in place.
The children touch him gently; the teacher lets him be.
                    Such a weight!
One black child in a perfect town;
there is no reason for sadness.

In an Urban School

The guard picks dead leaves from plants.
The sign over the table reads:
Do not take or *touch* anything on this table!
In the lunchroom the cook picks up in her dishcloth
what she refers to as "a little friend,"
shakes it out,
and puts the dishcloth back on the drain.
The teacher says she needs stronger tranquilizers.
Sweat rises on the bone of her nose,
on the plates of her skull under unpressed hair.
"First graders, put your heads down. I'm taking names
so I can tell your parents
which children do not obey their teacher."
Raheim's father was stabbed last week.
Germaine's mother, a junkie,
was found dead in an empty lot.

The Choice
(from a speech by Ellen Kuzwayo)

The children who were shot in Johannesburg
for throwing stones didn't pick the stones up
in Johannesburg. There are no
stones there—not even pebbles. They
filled their pockets in Soweto
and walked all the way.

Letter to Miss Glazer

Your face is creased from the lack of desire for beauty,
who never used oil or cold cream,
who never destroyed that icon, covered as if for a passion
    play,
by the hope for anything except for a good death;
who gave up on beauty in high school,
pimply, with flat-heeled shoes,
who gave up, a pitiful skinny lamb on the burning altar
    of repentance.
Where was that moment of witness?
In your bedroom, at the foot of your bed,
your hands clasped away from your tiny breasts?
Flattened by the weight of virginity, your shoes take you in
    straight lines:
you must go home and feed your mother;
tired, unable to think of anything but how the crust and
    cream smears around the cry of her mouth.
That mouth seems to suck up whatever is left, the last scrap
    God didn't want,
the one you saved in case something happened to change your
    life.

The Polishers of Brass

I am thinking of the men who polish brass in Georgetown;
bent over, their hands push back and forth with enormous
   force on each square inch.
So many doors, knobs, rails!
Men in their twenties, men in their sixties;
when they have gone all around and arrive at the place
   where they started, it has already tarnished, and they must
   begin again.

For the Dishwasher at Boothman's

I sit in front of him
and look him in the eye.
Pastrami on rye.

So accustomed to being invisible,
he startles, as if a door
opened and revealed his face.

His smile says, you should know better,
and he nods his head to the right
like a low angel would nod toward God.

His face is warped
around a center crack, as if
two pains were seamed
together at his birth.

His face would break
his mother's heart.

I read down the left side.
I read down the right.

Plaid Pants

At the bus terminal she says:
"Don't sit next to him,"
and she puts her finger next to her nose
to signal that
one dressed in that garment stinks.

He wears a long white robe,
like a priest with special orders—
the underwear of the Mass—
and a fur cap to cover
his wisdom, so it will stay hot
in this cold climate.
From the soiled seats heading toward Newark,
he stands up. Turning,
I see his face.
I smell nothing, but his face
has its own dark light
inside of the dark
of the cabin, like a moon,
or a candle under smoky glass.
He goes to the bathroom
and comes out a new man—
in plaid polyester pants!

Books

Today Lorca and Pound
fell off my shelf.
They lay there on the floor
like a couple of drunks.
How humble are the lives
of books!
How small their expectations!
They wait quietly,
pressed together,
to be called into
the light. When you open them,
they tell you everything
they know. They exhaust
you, like convicts
or madmen
too eager to talk.

Allen Ginsberg

Once Allen Ginsberg stopped to pee at a bookstore
  in New Jersey,
but he looked like a bum—
not like the miracle-laden Christ with electric atom juice,
  not like the one whose brain is a river in which was plunked
  the stone of the world (the one bathing fluid to wash away
  25,000 year half-lives), he was dressed as a bum.
He had wobbled on a pee-heavy bladder
in search of a gas station,
a dime store with a quarter booth,
a Chinese restaurant,
when he came to that grocery store of dreams:
Chunks of Baudelaire's skin
glittered in plastic;
his eyes in sets, innocent
as the unhoused eyes of a butchered cow.
In a dark corner, Rimbaud's
genitals hung like jerky,
and the milk of Whitman's breasts
drifted in a carton, dry as talcum.
He wanted to pee and lay his head
on the cool stacks;
but the clerk took one look
and thought of the buttocks of clean businessmen squatting
  during lunch hour,
the thin flanks of pretty girls buying poetry for school.
Behind her, faintly,
the deodorized bathroom.
She was the one at the gate
protecting civilization.
He turned, walked to the gutter,
unzipped his pants, and peed.
Do you know who that was?

A man in the back came forth.
Soon she was known as
the woman in the store on Main
who said no to Allen Ginsberg;
and she is proud—
so proud she told this story
pointing to the spot outside, as if
still flowed that holy stream.

Whitman, Come Again to the Cities

"Burn high your fires, foundry chimneys!
Cast black shadows at nightfall!
Cast red and yellow light over the tops of the houses!"
                                                —Walt Whitman

Father who found this vibrant light
rising out of the fired stomach of the city, rising out of
    the fecund genitals,
come with me
to the new sad cities
laid out on the earth like a tortured soldier,
the skin pulled off his back,
his eyes empty, but alive.
Come with me down the abandoned streets—
vacant lots of weeds, tin cans and blown garbage,
black and blue eyes of the windows,
thin dogs walking stealthily, a new breed neither wild
    nor tame,
but like those young boys walking with a starved eye
that deciphers quickly what can be eaten and what will eat.
What do they celebrate entering through metal doors
    to buy whiskey?
Mutilated seeds of the workers
through whose loins passes rusty blood,
and women who carry dead white ingots in their bellies.
Young men stand on street corners,
their clothes expensive, their cars impractical, wildly
    colored; and they will do anything but
put a piece
of another piece
in a certain place.

On the Turning Up
of Unidentified Black Female Corpses

Mowing his three acres with a tractor,
a man notices something ahead—a mannequin—
he thinks someone threw it from a car. Closer
he sees it is the body of a black woman.

The medics come and turn her with pitchforks.
Her gaze shoots past him to nothing. Nothing
is explained. How many black women
have been turned up to stare at us blankly,

in weedy fields, off highways,
pushed out in plastic bags,
shot, knifed, unclothed partially, raped,
their wounds sealed with a powdery crust.

Last week on TV, a gruesome face, eyes bloated shut.
No one will say, "She looks like she's sleeping," ropes
of blue-black slashes at the mouth. Does anybody
know this woman? Will anyone come forth? Silence

like a backwave rushes into that field
where, just the week before, four other black girls
had been found. The gritty image hangs in the air
just a few seconds, but it strikes me,

a black woman, there is a question being asked
about my life. How can I
protect myself? Even if I lock my doors,
walk only in the light, someone wants me dead.

Am I wrong to think
if five white women had been stripped,
broken, the sirens would wail until
someone was named?

Is it any wonder I walk over these bodies
pretending they are not mine, that I do not know
the killer, that I am just like any woman—
if not wanted, at least tolerated.

Part of me wants to disappear, to pull
the earth on top of me. Then there is this part
that digs me up with this pen
and turns my sad black face to the light.

A Note on My Son's Face

I.

Tonight, I look, thunderstruck
at the gold head of my grandchild.
Almost asleep, he buries his feet
between my thighs;
his little straw eyes
close in the near dark.
I smell the warmth of his raw
slightly foul breath, the new death
waiting to rot inside him.
Our breaths equalize our heartbeats;
every muscle of the chest uncoils,
the arm bones loosen in the nest
of nerves. I think of the peace
of walking through the house,
pointing to the name of this, the name of that,
an educator of a new man.

Mother. Grandmother. Wise
Snake-woman who will show the way;
Spider-woman whose black tentacles
hold him precious. Or will tear off his head,
her teeth over the little husband,
the small fist clotted in trust at her breast.

This morning, looking at the face of his father,
I remembered how, an infant, his face was too dark,
nose too broad, mouth too wide.
I did not look in that mirror
and see the face that could save me
from my own darkness.
Did he, looking in my eye, see
what I turned from:
my own dark grandmother
bending over gladioli in the field,

her shaking black hand defenseless
at the shining cock of flower?

I wanted that face to die,
to be reborn in the face of a white child.

I wanted the soul to stay the same,
for I loved to death,
to damnation and God-death,
the soul that broke out of me.
I crowed: My Son! My Beautiful!
But when I peeked in the basket,
I saw the face of a black man.

Did I bend over his nose
and straighten it with my fingers
like a vine growing the wrong way?
Did he feel my hand in malice?

Generations we prayed and fucked
for this light child,
the shining god of the second coming;
we bow down in shame
and carry the children of the past
in our wallets, begging forgiveness.

II.

A picture in a book,
a lynching.
The bland faces of men who watch
a Christ go up in flames, smiling,
as if he were a hooked
fish, a felled antelope, some
wild thing tied to boards and burned.
His charring body
gives off light—a halo

burns out of him.
His face scorched featureless;
the hair matted to the scalp
like feathers.
One man stands with his hand on his hip,
another with his arm
slung over the shoulder of a friend,
as if this moment were large enough
to hold affection.

III.

How can we wake
from a dream
we are born into,
that shines around us,
the terrible bright air?

Having awakened,
having seen our own bloody hands,
how can we ask forgiveness,
bring before our children the real
monster of their nightmares?

The worst is true.
Everything you did not want to know.

About the Author

Toi Derricotte was born in Hamtramck, Michigan, in 1941. She studied special education at Wayne State University, where she earned a B.A., and studied English literature and creative writing at New York University, where she received her M.A. She has won fellowships in poetry from the National Endowment for the Arts, the New Jersey State Council on the Arts, the Maryland State Arts Council, and was a MacDowell fellow in 1984. Her previous collections of poetry are *The Empress of the Death House* and *Natural Birth*. She lives in Norfolk, Virginia, and is Assistant Professor of English Literature at Old Dominion University.

PITT POETRY SERIES

Ed Ochester, General Editor